Playful Pet Projects

Get Crafting for Your
COOL CAT

by Ruth Owen

BEARPORT PUBLISHING

Minneapolis, Minnesota

CREATE!

Credits

Cover, © Okssi/Shutterstock, © Kasefoto/Shutterstock, and Ruby Tuesday Books; 1, © Ruby Tuesday Books and © Fedotov Anatoly/Shutterstock; 3, © Shutterstock; 4T, © Ruby Tuesday Books and © Fedotov Anatoly/Shutterstock; 4C, © Kasefoto/Shutterstock and Ruby Tuesday Books; 4B, © Csaba Vanyi/Shutterstock and Ruby Tuesday Books; 5T, © Halyna Tymochko/Shutterstock and Ruby Tuesday Books; 5B, © Anurak Pongpatimet/Shutterstock; 6, © Merydolla/Shutterstock and Mariesacha/Shutterstock; 7, © Ruby Tuesday Books; 8, © Ruby Tuesday Books; 9T, © Ruby Tuesday Books; 9B, © Ruby Tuesday Books and © Fedotov Anatoly/Shutterstock; 10, © Mariesacha/Shutterstock, © Kasefoto/Shutterstock, and Ruby Tuesday Books; 11, © Shutterstock and © Ruby Tuesday Books; 12, © Shutterstock and © Ruby Tuesday Books; 13, © Shutterstock and © Ruby Tuesday Books; 14, © Ruby Tuesday Books, © Csaba Vanyi/Shutterstock, and © PonomarenkoNataly/Shutterstock; 15, © Ruby Tuesday Books; 16, © Ruby Tuesday Books; 17, © Ruby Tuesday Books; 18T, © Halyna Tymochko/Shutterstock and © Ruby Tuesday Books; 18B, © Jrossphoto/Shutterstock; 19, © Ruby Tuesday Books; 20T, © gillmar/Shutterstock and © Yevtushenko Serhii/Shutterstock; 20B, © Ruby Tuesday Books; 21, © Ruby Tuesday Books; 22, © Africa Studio/Shutterstock, © Susan Schmitz/Shutterstock, © Kanowa/Shutterstock, and © Myimages–Micha/Shutterstock; 23, © Nynke van Holten/Shutterstock.

Library of Congress Cataloging-in-Publication Data

Names: Owen, Ruth, 1967– author.
Title: Get crafting for your cool cat / by Ruth Owen.
Description: Create! books. | Minneapolis, Minnesota : Bearport Publishing Company, [2021] | Series: Playful pet projects | Includes bibliographical references and index.
Identifiers: LCCN 2020030854 (print) | LCCN 2020030855 (ebook) | ISBN 9781647476601 (library binding) | ISBN 9781647476670 (ebook)
Subjects: LCSH: Handicraft. | Cats in art.
Classification: LCC TT157 .O854 2021 (print) | LCC TT157 (ebook) | DDC 745.5—dc23
LC record available at https://lccn.loc.gov/2020030854
LC ebook record available at https://lccn.loc.gov/2020030855

© 2021 Bearport Publishing Company. All rights reserved. No part of this publication may be reproduced in whole or in part, stored in any retrieval system, or transmitted in any form or by any means, electronic, mechanical, photocopying, recording, or otherwise, without written permission from the publisher.

For more information, write to Bearport Publishing, 5357 Penn Avenue South, Minneapolis, MN 55419. Printed in the United States of America.

CONTENTS

Get Crafty with Your Kitty! 4

Home Sweet Home
    A Cozy Pyramid Hideaway 6

Pet Snacks and Treats
    A Kitty Grass Planter 10

Time to Play
    Puzzle Foraging Board 14

Dress It Up
    A Kitty-Sized Mane 18

Top Tips for a Healthy, Happy Cat 22
Glossary 23
Index 24
Read More 24
Learn More Online 24
About the Author 24

GET CRAFTY WITH YOUR KITTY!

If you love spending time with your cat and you also enjoy making things, this is the *purr*fect book for you! Discover four fantastic craft projects that are fun to make and will give you and your cat hours of enjoyment.

◀ Home Sweet Home
Make your cat a space where it can feel safe. This pyramid hideaway will give your cat a place to feel calm and secure.

Pet Snacks and Treats ▶
Even though your cat is a **carnivore**, eating a little grass now and then is good for its **digestive system**. Learn how to grow kitty grass and turn a used plastic bottle into a cat-shaped planter.

◀ Time to Play
Help your cat keep its brain and body active. This easy-to-make puzzle **foraging** board will turn eating some treats into a challenging and exciting activity for your pet.

◀ **Dress It Up**
Make this lion's mane costume and have fun playing dress-up with your own little lion king or queen.

Have Fun and Be Safe

Crafting for your best **feline** friend can be lots of fun. But it's important that both you and your cat stay safe by following these top tips for careful crafting.

- Always get permission from an adult before making the projects in this book.
- Read the instructions carefully, and ask an adult for help if there's something you don't understand.
- Be careful when using scissors, and never let your cat touch or play with them.
- Keep any paint or glue where your cat can't sniff, lick, or touch it.

- When your project is complete, recycle any extra paper, cardboard, or packaging, and keep leftover materials for a future project.
- Clean up when you've finished working.
- Remember! Some cats do well with lots of touching, playing, and attention. But others only spend a little time with their humans.

Never force your cat to do something it seems unhappy to do.

Home Sweet Home
A COZY PYRAMID HIDEAWAY

Ancient Egyptians loved cats and kept them as pets. People in ancient Egypt even worshipped a cat goddess named Bastet. So what could be more perfect for your little cat god or goddess than a cozy, pyramid-shaped hideaway?

You will need
- A large piece of thick paper
- A pencil
- A yardstick
- Scissors
- 5 pieces of corrugated cardboard that are at least 18 inches (46 cm) square
- An adult helper
- Packing tape
- Colored paper
- Glue

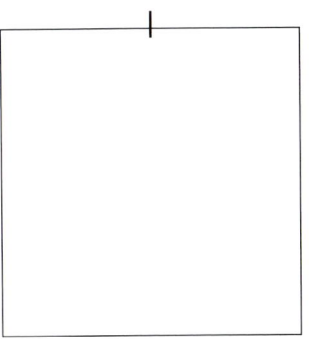

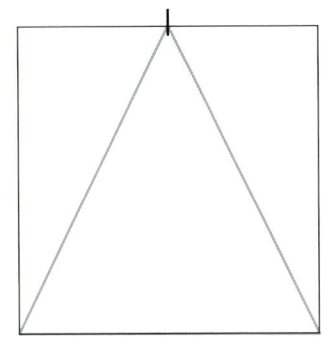

1 Begin by making a paper **template** for the sides of the pyramid. On the piece of thick paper, draw an 18 in (46 cm) square. Next, measure and mark the middle point on the top edge of the square.

Draw a line from the mark to each bottom corner. Carefully cut out the triangle.

2 Trace the template onto four pieces of cardboard and ask your adult helper to cut out the triangles.

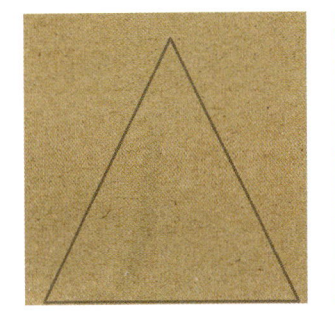

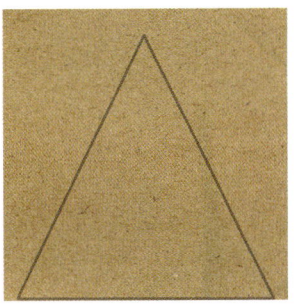

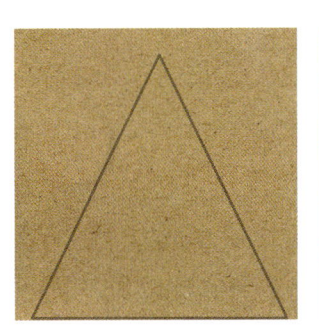

Template

Corrugated cardboard can be difficult to cut, so ask an adult to help.

3 On your fifth piece of cardboard, measure and draw an 18 in (46 cm) square. Ask your helper to cut out the square. This will be the base of your pyramid.

4 To make an entrance to the pyramid, measure and draw a square in the center of the bottom edge of one triangle. Have your helper cut it out.

> The opening should be big enough for your cat to get into the pyramid.

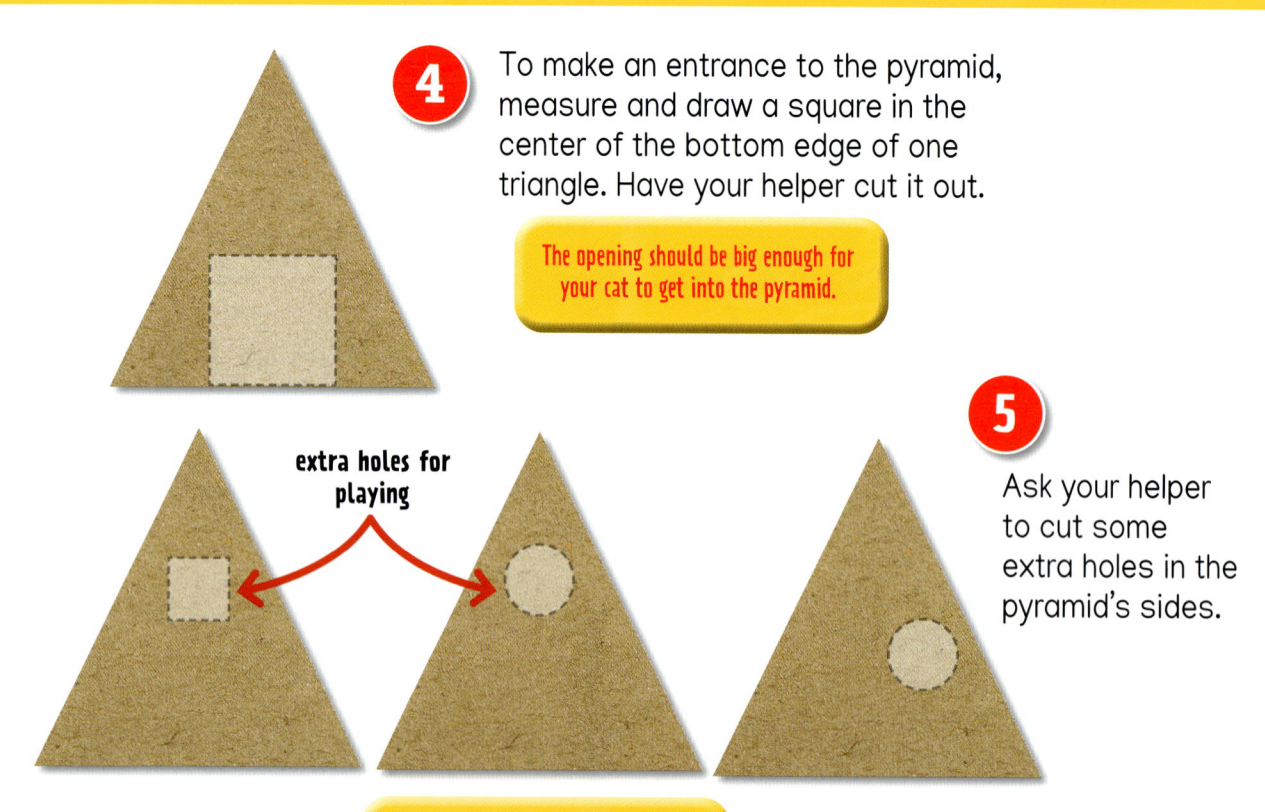

extra holes for playing

5 Ask your helper to cut some extra holes in the pyramid's sides.

> You can dangle toys into these holes for your cat to play with.

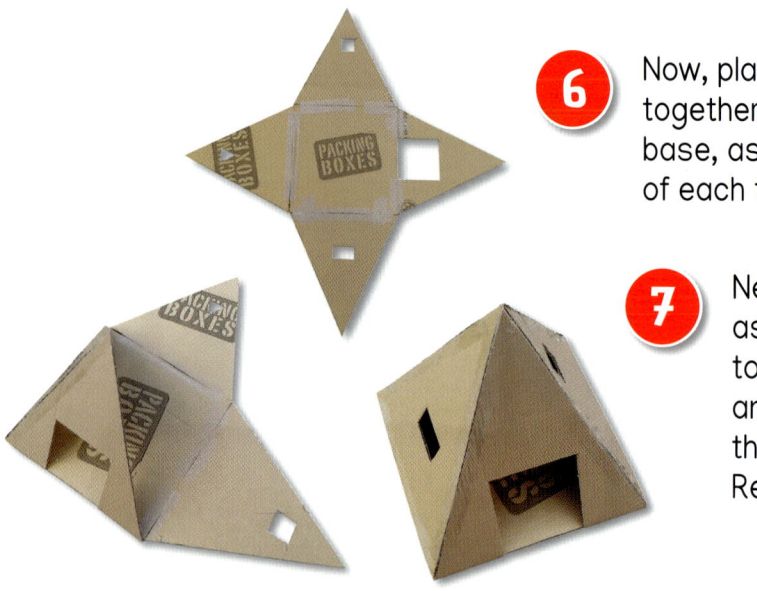

6 Now, place the five pieces of the pyramid together with the triangles around the base, as shown. Tape the bottom edge of each triangle to the square.

7 Next, fold up two triangles and ask a helper to hold them tightly together so their edges line up and they meet at the top. Tape the two triangles together. Repeat with all triangle sides.

8 Decorate your pyramid with paper shapes to look like the bricks of the Egyptian pyramids. Cut paper into small rectangles. This is a great way to recycle paper scraps left over from other crafting projects!

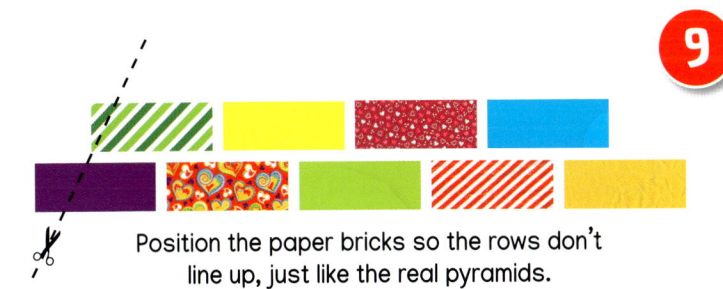

You can make your pyramid as colorful as you like!

9 Glue the paper rectangles in rows on each side of the pyramid. When you get to the end of each row, carefully trim the extra paper.

Position the paper bricks so the rows don't line up, just like the real pyramids.

10 When the glue has dried, put a cozy blanket inside and introduce your cat to its new pyramid hideaway.

Time for a nap!

Pet Snacks and Treats
A KITTY GRASS PLANTER

Munching on some grass helps cats spit up things they can't digest—such as their own furballs. Make a cute cat-shaped planter filled with special kitty grass that will help keep your cat's stomach healthy.

You will need
- An empty 2-liter plastic bottle
- A measuring tape
- A black marker
- An adult helper
- Scissors
- A sheet of colorful crafting foam
- A pencil
- Colored pens or markers
- Tacky glue
- Potting soil
- Cat grass seeds
- A saucer or large plastic lid
- A small watering can

Recycle this section.

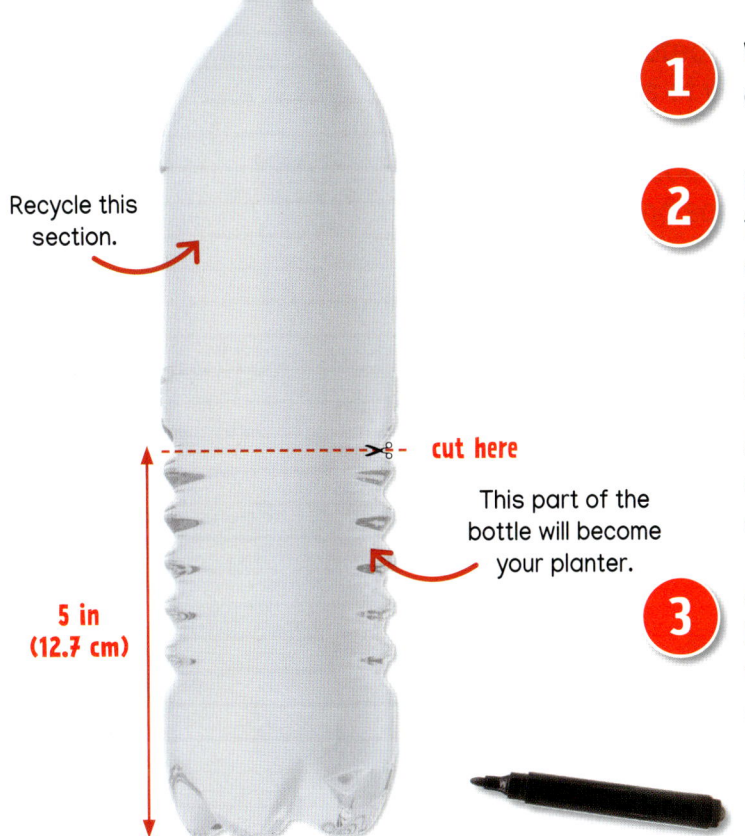

cut here

This part of the bottle will become your planter.

5 in (12.7 cm)

1 Wash out the plastic bottle and remove the label.

2 Measure 5 in (12.7 cm) up from the base of the bottle and make a mark. Repeat this in three more places on the bottle and then connect your marks with a line.

Ask an adult to help you cut around the line. Carefully trim off any sharp edges.

3 Ask an adult to poke three holes in the bottom of the planter to allow water to drain through.

4 Next, measure around the bottle. This measurement will be the length of the piece of foam you will use to cover your bottle.

Draw a rectangle on your foam that is 5 in (12.7 cm) high and the length of your measurement.

At the top of your rectangle, draw two cat's ears. Carefully cut out the foam.

11

5 Using the clean side of the foam where there are no pencil marks, draw your cat's face.

The soft foam edge will be safe for your cat when it is eating.

6 Wrap the foam around the bottle so that it is about ½ in (1.25 cm) higher than the edge of the bottle. Glue the foam in place.

12

Cat grass seeds

7 Fill the planter with potting soil, leaving about 1 in (2.5 cm) of room at the top of the planter.

Next, sprinkle some grass seeds on the surface of the soil. Cover the seeds with another thin layer of soil. Gently press down the soil with your fingers, and water the seeds until soil is **moist**.

Place the planter on a saucer or plastic lid, and put it in a warm, sunny place.

Remember to water the grass. The soil should feel moist but not soggy.

8 After about 10 days, the grass will be ready for your cat to eat.

Put the planter where your cat can reach it. After your cat has finished eating, put the planter out of the way!

Always follow any feeding instructions on the cat grass seed packet.

Saucer

Happy Munching!

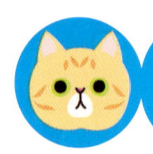

Time to Play
PUZZLE FORAGING BOARD

The **ancestors** of your cat were wild animals that hunted for food. Even though your pet no longer needs to hunt, foraging for treats on a puzzle board will help keep its mind and body active and healthy. The puzzle board has six different activities, or **modules**—try adding a new activity to the puzzle board each week.

The puzzle board can be used to feed treats or your cat's regular dry food. But make sure you do not overfeed your cat.

You will need
- A thick sheet of cardboard about 30 in x 18 in (76 cm x 46 cm) for the base of the puzzle board
- Recycled materials
- Cat treats or dry food

You will need
- A small plastic tub
- Scraps of recycled paper
- Glue

1 To make the lucky dip, scrunch up pieces of paper into small balls. Fill the tub with the paper balls and add a few treats.

2 Finally, glue the tub to the puzzle board.

Rustle the paper balls to get your cat's attention, and let your cat see you drop the treats into the tub.

Always stay with your cat when it's playing with the puzzle board. Pay attention to make sure your cat is not eating parts of the toy.

You will need
- About 20 plastic bottle tops
- Glue

1 To make bottle top snakes, glue 10 bottle tops to the puzzle board in a curvy line. Be sure the open part of the bottle tops face up so that treats can be put inside.

2 Glue on a second line of bottle tops about 1 in (2.5 cm) from the first. The second line should follow the shape of the first.

Put a treat in some of the bottle tops and two or three between the snakes.

You will need

- A small cardboard box (with all six sides intact) that is about 4 in (10 cm) high
- A toilet paper tube
- A marker
- Scissors
- An adult helper

1 Begin by tracing the end of the toilet paper tube to make circles on the top of the puzzle box. Then, trace some half circles along the bottom edges of the box. Ask an adult to help you carefully cut out the circles and half circles.

2 Glue the box to the puzzle board.

Let your cat see you drop treats inside. Your cat can try to grab them from the top and through the sides!

You will need

- Aluminum foil
- Glue

1 To make the silver spiral, take some aluminum foil and scrunch it into a rope that's about 50 in (127 cm) long and about ¾ in (2 cm) thick.

2 Now, curl the foil into a spiral. There should be about 1 in (2.5 cm) of space between each coil. Glue the spiral to the puzzle board.

Drop treats into the spiral.

You will need

- A small cardboard or plastic box about 4 in (7.5 cm) deep
- Toilet paper tubes
- Glue

When making modules for your puzzle board, always make sure there are no staples in boxes or sharp edges when you've finished cutting.

1 For the toilet tube trap, figure out how many toilet paper tubes will fit standing up in the box. Carefully cut them to the height of the box.

2 Squeeze the tubes into the box, and then glue the box to the puzzle board.

Drop treats into the tubes. Your cat will have to work hard to get them out!

You will need

- 5 paper towel tubes
- A small piece of paper
- A pencil
- Scissors
- Glue
- An adult helper

Try positioning the tubes so that the treats might fall from one to another as your cat grabs them with its paws!

1 Begin by making a circle template. Stand one tube upright on a piece of paper, trace around it, and then cut out the circle. Now, use the template to trace two circles onto each paper towel tube. Ask an adult to help you cut out the circles.

2 Glue three tubes to the puzzle board. Then, glue the other three tubes on top to form a pyramid shape.

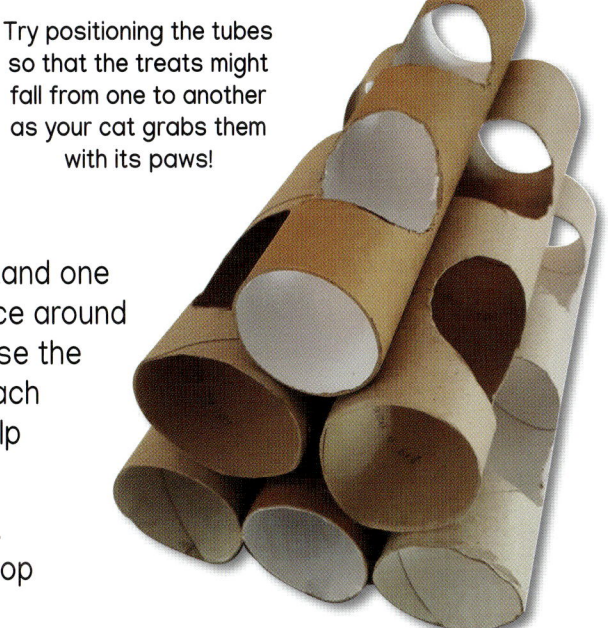

Dress It Up
A KITTY-SIZED MANE

Your pet cat belongs to the same animal family as leopards, tigers, and lions. You can't keep a lion as a pet. But you can turn your cat into a magnificent mini lion by making this kitty-sized mane!

You will need
- Tracing paper
- A pencil
- Scissors
- 2 sheets of paper
- A small clip
- A tape measure
- A glue stick
- Long fake fur
- Sewing pins
- Thread (in a color to match the fur)
- A needle
- A small piece of self-adhesive Velcro

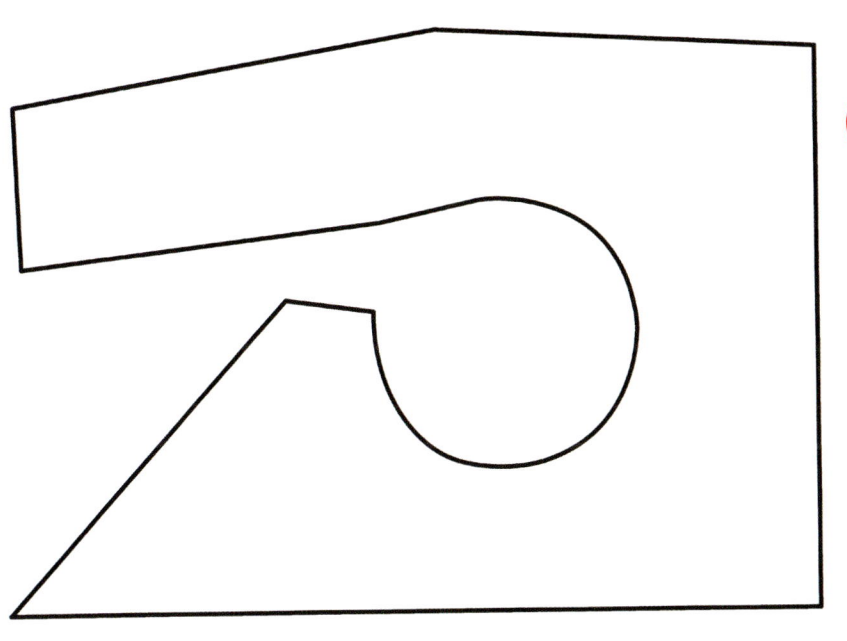

1. To make a template for your lion's mane, begin by tracing the shape from this page onto tracing paper and cutting it out.

2. Fold a sheet of paper in half so the short sides meet. Clip the template from step 1 along the folded edge of the paper, as shown. Trace around the shape and then remove the template.

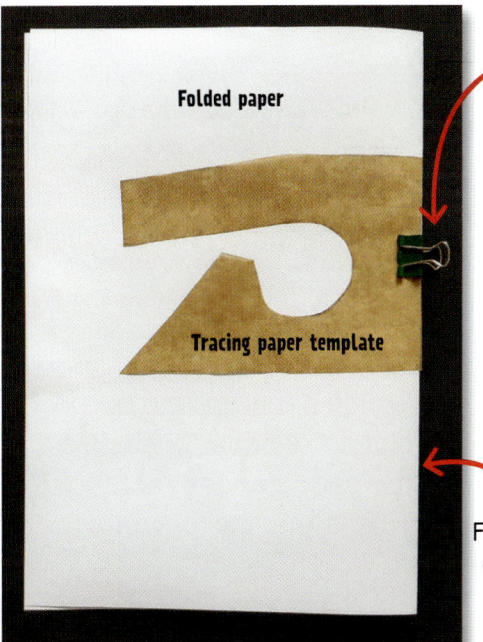

A small clip holds the template in place.

Folded paper

Tracing paper template

Folded edge

3. Cut out the shape you've just traced, being sure to cut through both layers of paper. Unfold the shape.

4 Next, gently measure your cat's head. Measure behind the ears and around the face under the chin and back up to where you started.

The tape measure should be loose.

5 On a fresh sheet of paper, draw a rectangle that is 3 in (7.5 cm) wide and the length of your cat's head measurement plus one extra inch. Cut out the rectangle.

Measure and mark the halfway line on the rectangle.

6 Place the cutout you just made onto the rectangle so it is centered along the halfway point of the rectangle. Use a tiny dab of glue to hold the papers together.

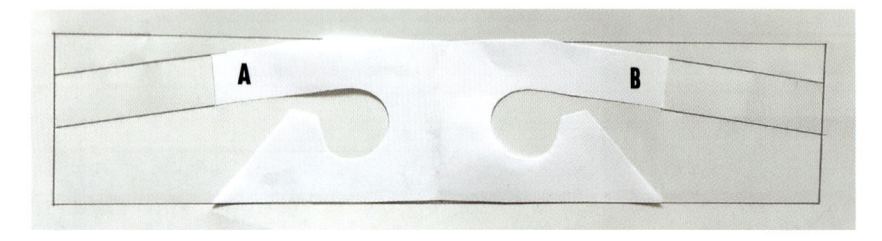

Now, trace around the template and draw lines that extend the sections labeled A and B to the ends of the rectangle.

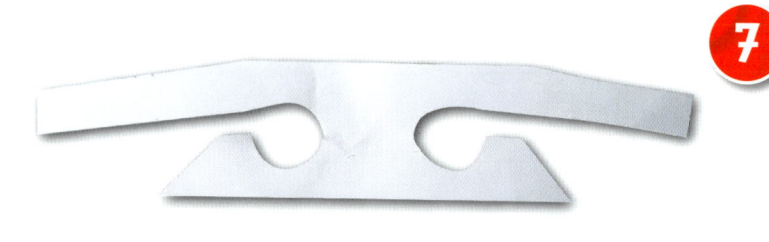

7 Gently separate the two pieces of paper and cut out the shape on the rectangle. This is the final **pattern**.

8 Carefully pin the pattern to the back of the fur fabric. Then, cut around the pattern.

9 Sew the two bottom sections of fabric to the top sections. As you do this, the area around the ear holes will curve into a rounded shape that will fit onto your cat's head. Finally, stick the Velcro fastenings to the ends of the mane.

Pieces of Velcro

Only dress up your cat for a few minutes and stop if it seems upset.

Only try your cat costume indoors, and never leave your cat alone when it is wearing its mane.

PURR!
MEOW!
ROAR!

TOP TIPS FOR A HEALTHY, HAPPY CAT!

Being a **responsible** cat owner is all about keeping your pet healthy and happy. Here are 10 tips to help you take care of your cat.

1. If your cat eats too much, it can become overweight and unhealthy. Ask your vet how much your cat should eat.

Healthy cat    **Overweight cat**

2. Wash your cat's food bowl every day.

3. Wash your cat's water bowl and refill it with fresh water every day.

4. Cats often do best with a routine, so try to feed your cat at the same time each day.

5. Alcohol, onions, chocolate, human medicines, and lilies are all very dangerous to your pet. Keep these things away from your cat.

6. Brush your cat once or twice a week.

7. Cats need to scratch to stay healthy. Buy or build your cat a scratching post.

8. Give your cat plenty of toys. A recycled cardboard box, paper bag, or ball of paper are free for you and fun for your cat.

9. Cats can climb up high. Create a bed or hiding place that your cat can get to on a high shelf.

10. Some cats seek out lots of petting, but others don't. To be sure your pet is happy, think **C.A.T.**

   C is for Choice
   Let your cat choose when it wants to be touched.

   A is for Attention
   Pay attention. Is it enjoying being petted or is it getting uncomfortable?

   T is for Touch
   Watch carefully to learn if your cat likes to be touched and how much.

GLOSSARY

ancestors family members who lived a long time ago

ancient Egyptians people who lived in Egypt, in Africa, from 5,000 to about 2,000 years ago

carnivore an animal that eats only meat

digestive system the stomach, intestines, and other body parts that work together to break down food in an animal's or a person's body

feline a cat or other member of the cat family

foraging looking for food in the wild

modules individual parts of something; often modules fit together

moist damp or slightly wet

pattern a shape that is used as a guide in crafts

responsible caring, trustworthy, and in charge

template a shape that can be used for drawing and cutting around

INDEX

ancient Egyptians 6
Bastet 6
costume 5, 21
digest 4, 10
eating 4, 12–13, 15, 22
fur 10, 18, 21–22
hideaways 4, 6, 9
kitty grass 4, 10, 13

lions 5, 18–19, 21
petting 22
playing 4–5, 8, 13–15, 17
pyramids 4, 6–9, 17
recycled materials 5, 9, 11, 14–15, 22
safety 4–5, 12, 17
toys 8, 15, 22

READ MORE

Bates, Cyril. *I Want to Draw Cats (Learn to Draw!)*. New York: PowerKids Press, 2019.

Felix, Rebecca. *Cats, Cats, Cats! (Internet Animal Stars)*. Minneapolis: Lerner Publications, 2021.

LEARN MORE ONLINE

1. Go to www.factsurfer.com
2. Enter "**Crafting Cat**" into the search box.
3. Click on the cover of this book to see a list of websites.

ABOUT THE AUTHOR

Ruth Owen has been developing and writing children's books for more than 10 years. She lives in Cornwall, England, just minutes from the ocean. Ruth thinks cats are the best thing in the world and lives with three feline friends named Harry, Bessie, and Tash (who was named for her furry white mustache).